AMAZING ANIMAL Q&AS

WHY ARE FLAMINGOS PINK?

by Nancy Dickmann

Raintree is an imprint of Capstone Global Library Limited, a company incorporated having its registered office at 264 Banbury Road, Oxford, OX2 7DY – Registered 6695582

www.raintree.co.uk
myorders@raintree.co.uk

Text © Capstone Global Library Limited 2022
The moral rights of the proprietor have been asserted.

All rights reserved. No part of this publication may be reproduced in any form or by any means (including photocopying or storing it in any medium by electronic means and whether or not transiently or incidentally to some other use of this publication) without the written permission of the copyright owner, except in accordance with the provisions of the Copyright, Designs and Patents Act 1988 or under the terms of a licence issued by the Copyright Licensing Agency, 5th Floor, Shackleton House, 4 Battle Bridge Lane, London SE1 2HX (www.cla.co.uk). Applications for the copyright owner's written permission should be addressed to the publisher.

Edited by Megan Peterson
Designed by Ted Williams
Original illustrations © Capstone Global Library Limited 2022
Picture research by Jo Miller
Production by Spencer Rosio
Originated by Capstone Global Library Ltd
Printed and bound in India

978 1 3982 1561 0 (hardback)
978 1 3982 1569 6 (paperback)

British Library Cataloguing in Publication Data
A full catalogue record for this book is available from the British Library.

Acknowledgements
We would like to thank the following for permission to reproduce photographs: Capstone Studio: Karon Dubke, 20; iStockphoto: Siddharthmitra9, 11; Shutterstock: BeeRu, Cover, Binh Thanh Bui, 18, Bohdana Seheda, design element, GUDKOV ANDREY, 7, Kanokratnok, 9, Keyur Athaide, 19, Marten_House, 13, Ondrej Prosicky, 4, owatta, design element, pp1, 8, Sunit Das, 15, tristan tan, 20-21 (birds), Weblogiq, 17, WitR, 5, Wolfgang Kruck, 16

Every effort has been made to contact copyright holders of material reproduced in this book. Any omissions will be rectified in subsequent printings if notice is given to the publisher.

All the internet addresses (URLs) given in this book were valid at the time of going to press. However, due to the dynamic nature of the internet, some addresses may have changed, or sites may have changed or ceased to exist since publication. While the author and publisher regret any inconvenience this may cause readers, no responsibility for any such changes can be accepted by either the author or the publisher.

CONTENTS

Pretty in pink 4

Spot the difference 6

Time for dinner 8

What's on the menu? 10

Colour magic 12

Pink all over 14

Are flamingos always pink? 16

You are what you eat 18

    Make a bird rainbow 20

    Glossary 22

    Find out more 23

    Index 24

Words in **bold** are in the glossary.

Pretty in pink

It's hard to miss a flamingo. These birds walk on long, skinny legs. They have S-shaped necks. They have curving **bills**. And they are pink!

Flamingos live in many places. They are found in warm areas. They stay near shallow lakes. Their large groups are called **flocks**. But why are they pink?

Spot the difference

There's something different about this baby flamingo. Can you spot it? It's not pink! Baby flamingos are white or grey when they hatch. They have soft, fuzzy **down**.

It takes a few years for a baby to grow into an adult. In that time, it gets taller. Its eyes change from dark grey to yellow. And something happens to turn its feathers pink.

7

Time for dinner

A bird that turns pink is strange. A flamingo's bill is strange too! In most birds, only the bottom part of the beak moves. In a flamingo, the top part moves. Why? The flamingo eats with its head upside down!

Soft, comb-like hairs line its bill. The flamingo sucks in water. Then it pushes the water out. The hairs keep food trapped inside.

What's on the menu?

What's the secret of a flamingo's colour? Its food! Flamingos eat blue-green **algae**. These tiny **cells** are like plants. Flamingos eat **shrimp** too. They also eat insects and small fish.

Pigments give things colour. One pigment makes things red, yellow or orange. It is found in carrots. It's in tomatoes too. It is also in algae and other flamingo food.

11

Colour magic

Blue-green algae aren't pink. Shrimp aren't pink either. But when they end up in a flamingo's stomach, something like magic happens.

The food is broken down. Red-orange pigments in the food mix with the flamingo's body **fats**. These fats end up in the bird's feathers. And that turns the feathers pink!

13

Pink all over

Most flamingos have pink legs. Their feet are pink too. Their pink legs are skinny. They are also very long. They let a flamingo wade into deep water.

Flamingos often stand on one leg. They tuck one foot under their bodies. This keeps the foot warm. On one leg, they sway in the wind. They have very good balance!

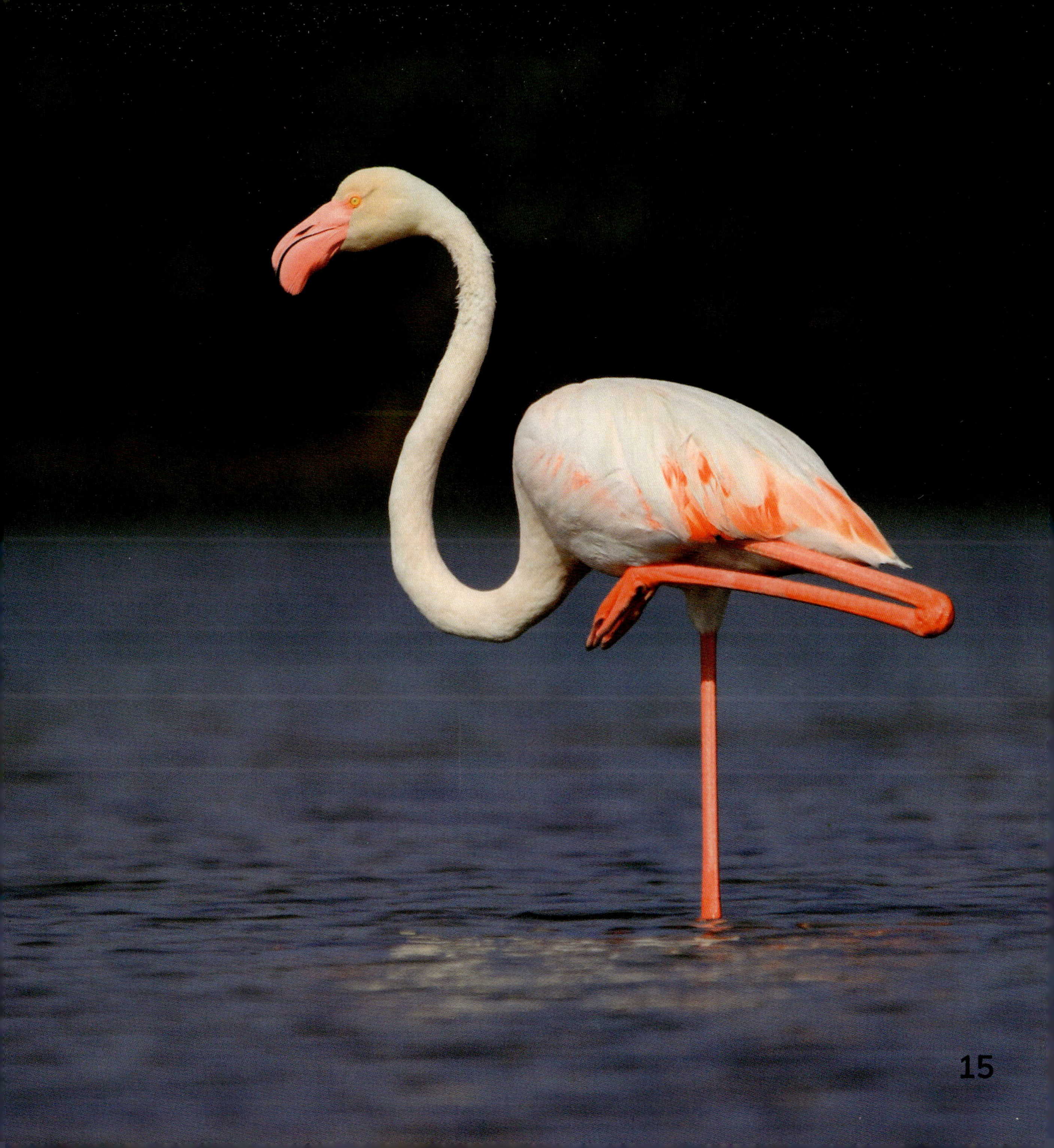

Are flamingos always pink?

There are different types of flamingos. They eat slightly different things. This makes some of them pinker than others. One type is pale pink. Another is almost red.

A flamingo's colour can change. They must keep eating foods that make them pink. If they don't, they will lose their pink colour. Flamingos in zoos eat special food to stay pink.

You are what you eat

People can change colour too! We eat fruit and vegetables. Many have the same pigments as flamingo food. Too much can make our skin change. It can look yellow or orange.

Don't try this at home! Eating just one or two foods works for some animals. But it's not good for humans. We need to eat many different foods. We're not flamingos!

Make a bird rainbow

What you need:
- nature magazines
- computer and printer
- scissors
- paper
- tape or glue

What to do:

1. Find pictures of different birds. Look in magazines and on the internet. Try to find birds in every colour of the rainbow.

2. Cut or print out the photos.

3. Arrange them in rainbow order. Tape or glue them in place.

4. Display your bird rainbow!

Glossary

algae simple plant-like living things that live in the sea and freshwater

bill hard front part of the mouth of birds; also called a beak

cell tiny structure that makes up all living things

down soft, fluffy feathers of a bird

fat oily substance found in the bodies of animals and some plants

flock group of the same type of animal; members of flocks live, travel and eat together

pigment substance that gives something a particular colour when it is present or added

shrimp small sea animal with a hard shell and long tail

Find out more

Books

Birds (DKFindout!), DK (DK Children, 2019)

Brilliant Birds (Extreme Animals), Isabel Thomas (Raintree, 2012)

Why Do Owls and Other Birds Have Feathers? (Animal Body Coverings), Holly Beaumont (Raintree, 2016)

Websites

www.bbc.co.uk/bitesize/topics/z6882hv
Learn more about animals, from mammals to minibeasts.

www.dkfindout.com/uk/animals-and-nature/animal-kingdom
Find out more about the animal kingdom.

Index

algae 10, 12

bills 4, 8, 9

down 6

eating 8, 9, 10, 12, 16, 17, 19

eyes 6

feathers 6, 12

flocks 5

legs 4, 14

necks 4

pigments 10, 12, 18

shrimp 10, 12

water 5, 9, 14

young 6